Writing and Using
Learning Outcomes

The challenge to designers of curricula in higher education is now to harness the use of learning outcomes to view learning from the perspective of the learner, rather than the lecture, and thereby to enrich the quality of learning experienced by undergraduate students.

(Allan, J., 1996)

1. Introduction

2. What are Learning Outcomes?

3. How do I write Learning Outcomes?

Acknowledgements

The idea for this handbook arose from a seminar held with the staff of UCC who were participating in the *Postgraduate Certificate / Diploma in Teaching and Learning in Higher Education*. It was clear from the feedback that busy staff members did not have time to read the long list of books and journal articles that I had recommended. They required a short, clear and readable handbook to guide them on their journey through the concept of learning outcomes. I was not aware of any such publication and, thanks to the encouragement of Professor Áine Hyland and Dr Norma Ryan, I began the task of writing this handbook. Without their help and support, this work could never have been completed.

I wish to acknowledge the receipt of a grant from the Higher Education Authority, funded under the National Development Plan 2000 – 2006, via the Quality Promotion Committee of University College Cork to cover the costs involved in producing this handbook.

A special word of thanks to my colleagues who read and made such helpful comments on the initial manuscript: Dr Mike Cosgrove, Cynthia Deane, Eleanor Fouhy, Randal Henly, Dr Bettie Higgs, Professor Áine Hyland, Marian McCarthy, Dr Norma Ryan and Dr Anna Ridgway.

I also wish to thank Paula Duane and Brigid Farrell who were of great assistance in sourcing many of the literature references listed in this handbook. Thanks also to the Boole Library staff, particularly those in the Inter-Library Loans section, who were extremely helpful at all stages of this project. I wish to thank the members of staff of UCC who participated in the *Postgraduate Certificate / Diploma in Teaching and Learning in Higher Education* and who wrote the learning outcomes listed in Appendix 2. The fact that I could draw on exemplars from a wide range of subjects across the university has been of great assistance to me. Last, but by no means least, sincere thanks to the staff at Design Matters for their super efficiency when working on the design and layout of this publication.

The term teacher rather than lecturer has been used throughout this handbook since it is my experience, both as a student and staff member in UCC, that this university has many outstanding and gifted teachers.

Declan Kennedy MSc, MEd, PhD, HDE, FICI
Department of Education, University College Cork.

Acronyms used

ECTS   European Credit Transfer System

EHEA   European Higher Education Area

ERA   European Research Area

QAA   Quality Assurance Agency for Higher Education, UK

SEEC   Southern England Consortium for Credit Accumulation and Transfer

Executive Summary

The overall aim of the Bologna Agreement (1999) is to improve the efficiency and effectiveness of higher education in Europe. One of the main features of this process is the need to improve the traditional ways of describing qualifications and qualification structures. As a step towards achieving greater clarity in the description of qualifications, by 2010 all modules and programmes in third level institutions throughout the European Union will be written in terms of learning outcomes.

International trends in education show a shift from the traditional *teacher-centred* approach to a *student-centred* approach, i.e. the focus is not only on teaching but also on what the students are expected to be able to do at the end of the module or programme. Statements called *learning outcomes* are used to express what the students are expected to achieve and how they are expected to demonstrate that achievement. Learning outcomes are defined as statements of what a learner is expected to know, understand and/or be able to demonstrate after completion of a process of learning (ECTS, 2005).

When writing learning outcomes it is helpful to make use of *Bloom's Taxonomy of Educational Objectives*. This classification or categorisation of levels of thinking behaviour provides a ready-made structure and list of verbs to assist in writing learning outcomes. Most learning outcomes describe evidence of learning in areas like knowledge, comprehension, application, analysis, synthesis and evaluation. This area is known as the *cognitive domain*. The other two main domains are the *affective domain* (attitudes, feelings, values) and the *psychomotor domain* (physical skills).

In general, when writing learning outcomes begin with an action verb followed by the object of that verb. This handbook contains a list of action verbs for each area of Bloom's Taxonomy. Sentences should be kept short to ensure clarity. Learning outcomes must be capable of being assessed. When deciding on the number of learning outcomes to write, the general recommendation in the literature is about six learning outcomes per module. The most common mistake in writing learning outcomes is to use vague terms like *know, understand, learn, be familiar with, be exposed to, be acquainted with* and *be aware of*.

It is important to link learning outcomes to teaching and learning activities and assessment. This may be done with the aid of a grid to assist in checking that the learning outcomes map on to the teaching and learning activities as well as to the mode of assessment.

The advantages of learning outcomes for teachers and students are well documented in the literature in terms of clarity, effectiveness of teaching and learning, curriculum design and assessment. In addition, learning outcomes assist greatly in the more systematic design of programmes and modules.

Chapter 1
Introduction

Learning outcomes are important for recognition ... The principal question asked of the student or the graduate will therefore no longer be "what did you do to obtain your degree?" but rather "what can you do now that you have obtained your degree?". This approach is of relevance to the labour market and is certainly more flexible when taking into account issues of lifelong learning, non-traditional learning, and other forms of non-formal educational experiences.
(Council of Europe, 2002)

1.1 Why this handbook?

The Bologna Process specifies that by 2010 all programmes and significant constituent elements of programmes in third level institutions throughout the European Union will be written in terms of learning outcomes. This handbook has been written to assist teachers in understanding and applying learning outcomes to the modules that they teach. Whilst it has been written specifically for the teaching and administrative staff of University College Cork, it is also hoped that it will be found helpful by teachers and administrators in other institutions and at all levels of education.

1.2 The Bologna Process

In June 1999, representatives of the Ministers of Education of EU member states convened in Bologna, Italy to formulate the Bologna Agreement leading to the setting up of a common European Higher Education Area (EHEA). The overall aim of the Bologna Process is to improve the efficiency and effectiveness of higher education in Europe. The agreement is designed so that the independence and autonomy of the universities and other third level institutions would ensure that higher education and research in Europe adapt to the changing needs of society and the advances in scientific knowledge (URL 1).

Bologna, Italy

Some of the key points arising from the Bologna Declaration and subsequent meetings may be summarised as follows:

- The European Higher Education Area (EHEA) will ensure the increased international competitiveness of the European system of higher education.

- The traditional ways of describing qualifications and qualification structures need to be improved and made more transparent. A system of easily readable and comparable degrees is being adopted.

- Every student graduating will receive a Diploma Supplement automatically and free of charge, in a widely-spoken European language. This supplement describes the qualification the student has received in a standard format that is easy to understand and compare. It also describes the content of the qualification and the structure of the higher education system within which it was issued. The purpose of the supplement is to improve transparency and facilitate recognition.

- The system of degrees will be comprised of two main cycles – the first cycle lasting a minimum of three years (now defined as a minimum of 180 credits) and the second cycle leading to the master's and/or doctor's degree. This was subsequently modified to include the doctoral level as a separate third cycle in the Bologna Process and to promote closer links between the European Higher Education Area (EHEA) and the European Research Area (ERA).

- The introduction of a transferable system of academic credits will assist in the promotion of mobility within the EHEA by overcoming legal recognitions and administrative obstacles.

- The transferable system of academic credits assists in promoting European co-operation in quality assurance.

- The position of higher education institutions and students as essential partners in the Bologna Process is confirmed.

- The European dimension in higher education will be promoted through inter-institutional co-operation, curricula and mobility schemes for students and teachers and researchers.

A number of follow-up meetings were held after the meeting in Bologna to move the process forward. The venues agreed for these meetings were Prague (2001), Berlin (2003), Bergen (2005) and London (2007). A communiqué is issued after each meeting.

At the Berlin meeting in 2003, the Ministers for Education issued a communiqué on the position of the Bologna Process. They emphasised the creation of a common model for Higher Education in Europe and specified that degrees (Bachelor and Masters) will be described in terms of learning outcomes, rather than simply number of hours of study:

> *Ministers encourage the member States to elaborate a framework of comparable and compatible qualifications for their higher education systems, which should seek to describe qualifications in terms of workload, level, learning outcomes, competences and profile. They also undertake to elaborate an overarching framework of qualifications for the European Higher Education Area.*
> (Berlin Communiqué 2003, URL 2)

1.3 The contribution of learning outcomes to the Bologna action lines

The Bologna Process spells out a number of "action lines" in which learning outcomes play an important role (Adam, 2004). The main action lines may be summarised as follows:

- **Adoption of a system of easily readable and comparable degrees.** The use of learning outcomes as a type of common language for describing qualifications helps to make these qualifications clearer to other institutions, employers and those involved in evaluating qualifications.

- **Promotion of mobility.** Since learning outcomes help to make qualifications more transparent, this facilitates student exchanges as the process of recognition of study carried out in other institutions will be made straightforward.

- **Establishment of a system of credits.** The European Credit Transfer System (ECTS) had developed from simply being a system for recognising study at foreign institutions into a Credit Transfer and Accumulation System that takes all learning into account – not just study in other countries. The ECTS system is based on the principle that 60 credits measure the workload of a full-time student during one academic year. In the ECTS Users' Guide (2005) the position of learning outcomes in the credit system is clearly stated: "Credits in ECTS can only be obtained after successful completion of the work required and appropriate assessment of the learning outcomes achieved" (ECTS Users' Guide, 2005, p.4). Adam (2004) summarises the situation very well when he says: "Credits expressed in terms of learning outcomes are a powerful way to recognise and quantify learning achievement from different contexts; they also provide an effective structure for relating qualifications. The addition of the learning outcomes dimension has the potential to improve dramatically the effectiveness of ECTS as a true pan-European system."

- **Promotion of co-operation in quality assurance.** The use of learning outcomes as a common method for describing programmes and modules has the potential to assist in the establishment of common standards and common methods of quality assurance between institutions. It is hoped that the increased confidence in the area of quality assurance between institutions will assist in the creation of the European Higher Education Area.

- **Promotion of the European dimension in higher education.** Since programmes will be expressed using the common terminology of learning outcomes, this greatly simplifies the development of joint degree programmes and integrated study programmes.

- **Lifelong learning.** The use of a credit-based system linked to learning outcomes has the potential to create a flexible and integrated system to assist people of all ages to gain educational qualifications. Without the introduction of learning outcomes, the system of lifelong learning in many countries will remain complicated and disjointed.

- **Higher education and students.** The use of learning outcomes when describing programmes and modules makes it very clear to students what they are expected to achieve by the end of the programme or module. This also assists students in the choice of programmes and in actively participating in student-centred learning.

The target date for full implementation of the Bologna Process is 2010. It is hoped that this handbook will assist you to begin the challenge of expressing modules and programmes in terms of learning outcomes.

Chapter 2
What are Learning Outcomes?

Learning outcomes represent one of the essential building blocks for transparent higher education systems and qualifications.

(Adam, 2004 p.3)

2.1 Introduction

The traditional way of designing modules and programmes was to start from the content of the course. Teachers decided on the content that they intended to teach on the programme, planned how to teach this content and then assessed the content. This type of approach focussed on the teacher's input and on the assessment in terms of how well the students absorbed the material. Course descriptions referred mainly to the content of the course that would be covered in lectures. This approach to teaching is commonly referred to as a **teacher-centred approach.** Among the criticisms of this type of approach in the literature (Gosling and Moon, 2001) is that it can be difficult to state precisely what the student has to be able to do in order to pass the module or programme.

International trends in education show a shift from the traditional "teacher-centred" approach to a "student-centred" approach. This alternative model focuses on what **the students** are expected to be able to do at the end of the module or programme. Hence, this approach is commonly referred to as an **outcome-based** approach. Statements called **intended learning outcomes,** commonly shortened to **learning outcomes,** are used to express what it is expected that students should be able to do at the end of the learning period. The term *learning outcome* will be defined more precisely in Section 2.2.

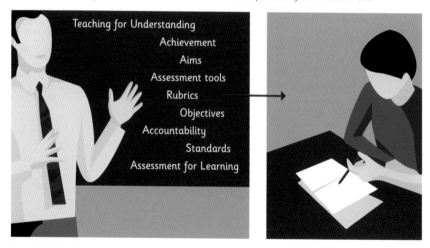

Fig. 2.1 Teacher-centred approaches place the emphasis on the teacher. Outcome-based approaches place the emphasis on the student.

The outcome-based approach can be traced back to the work of what is called the *behavioural objectives* movement of the 1960s and 1970s in the USA. Among the best known advocates of this type of teaching was Robert Mager who proposed the idea of writing very specific statements about observable outcomes. He called these statements *instructional objectives* (Mager, 1975). Using these instructional objectives and performance outcomes, he attempted to define the type of learning that would occur at the conclusion of instruction and how that learning would be assessed. These instructional objectives later developed into more precisely defined learning outcomes (Section 2.2).

Gosling and Moon (2001) point out the fact that the outcomes-based approach to teaching is becoming increasingly popular at an international level:

> *The outcome-based approach has been increasingly adopted within credit frameworks and by national quality and qualifications authorities such as the QAA (Quality Assurance Agency for Higher Education) in the UK, the Australian, New Zealand and South African Qualification Authorities*
> (Gosling and Moon, 2001)

With the implementation of the Bologna Process by 2010, all modules and programmes throughout the participating countries will be expressed using the outcomes-based approach, i.e. in terms of learning outcomes.

2.2 Defining learning outcomes

A survey of some of the literature in the area of learning outcomes shows a number of similar definitions:

Learning outcomes are statements of what is expected that the student will be able to do as a result of a learning activity.
(Jenkins and Unwin, 2001)

Learning outcomes are statements that specify what learners will know or be able to do as a result of a learning activity. Outcomes are usually expressed as knowledge, skills or attitudes.
(American Association of Law Libraries, URL 3)

Learning outcomes are an explicit description of what a learner should know, understand and be able to do as a result of learning.
(Bingham, 1999)

Learning outcomes are statements of what a learner is expected to know, understand and/or be able to demonstrate after completion of a process of learning.
(ECTS Users' Guide, 2005)

Learning outcomes are explicit statements of what we want our students to know, understand or be able to do as a result of completing our courses.
(University of New South Wales, Australia, URL 4)

Learning outcome: a statement of what a learner is expected to know, understand and/or be able to demonstrate at the end of a period of learning.
(Gosling and Moon, 2001)

A learning outcome is a statement of what the learner is expected to know, understand and/or be able to do at the end of a period of learning.
(Donnelly and Fitzmaurice, 2005)

A learning outcome is a statement of what a learner is expected to know, understand and be able to do at the end of a period of learning and of how that learning is to be demonstrated.
(Moon, 2002)

Learning outcomes describe what students are able to demonstrate in terms of knowledge, skills and attitudes upon completion of a program.
(Quality Enhancement Committee, Texas University, URL 5)

In a report written by Stephen Adam (Adam, 2004) on the United Kingdom Bologna seminar held in Edinburgh in 2004, a learning outcome was defined as:

A learning outcome is a written statement of what the successful student/learner is expected to be able to do at the end of the module/course unit or qualification.
(Adam, 2004)

Thus, we can see that the various definitions of learning outcomes do not differ significantly from each other. From the various definitions it is clear that:

- Learning outcomes focus on what the student has achieved rather than merely focussing on the content of what has been taught.

- Learning outcomes focus on what the student can demonstrate at the end of a learning activity.

The following definition (ECTS Users' Guide, p. 47) of a learning outcome may be considered a good working definition:

Learning outcomes are statements of what a student is expected to know, understand and/or be able to demonstrate after completion of a process of learning.

The process of learning could be, for example, a lecture, a module or an entire programme. Whilst it is common for teachers to plan learning outcomes for individual lessons or lectures, the emphasis in this handbook will be on writing learning outcomes for modules.

2.3 What is the difference between aims, objectives and learning outcomes?

The **aim** of a module or programme is a broad general statement of the teaching intention, i.e. it indicates what the teacher intends to cover in a block of learning. Aims are usually written from the teacher's point of view to indicate the general content and direction of the module. For example, the aim of a module could be "to introduce students to the basic principles of atomic structure" or "to provide a general introduction to the history of Ireland in the twentieth century".

The **objective** of a module or programme is usually a specific statement of teaching intention, i.e. it indicates one of the specific areas that the teacher intends to cover in a block of learning. For example, one of the objectives of a module could be that "students would understand the impacts and effects of behaviours and lifestyles on both the local and global environments". (In some contexts, objectives are also referred to as goals.)

Thus, the aim of a module gives the broad purpose or general teaching intention of the module whilst the objective gives more specific information about what the teaching of the module hopes to achieve.

One of the problems caused by the use of objectives is that sometimes they are written in terms of teaching intention and other times they are written in terms of expected learning, i.e. there is confusion in the literature in terms of whether objectives belong to the teacher-centred approach or the outcome-based approach. The situation is nicely summarised by Moon (2002) as follows:

> Basically the term 'objective' tends to complicate the situation, because objectives may be written in the terms of teaching intention or expected learning... This means that some descriptions are of the teaching in the module and some are of the learning... This general lack of agreement as to the format of objectives is a complication, and justifies the abandonment of the use of the term 'objective' in the description of modules or programmes.
> (Moon J., 2002)

Most teachers who have worked on the development of objectives for modules or programmes would have encountered the above problem. One of the great advantages of learning outcomes is that they are clear statements of what the student is expected to achieve and how he or she is expected to demonstrate that achievement. Thus, learning outcomes are more precise, easier to compose and far clearer than objectives. From one perspective, learning outcomes can be considered as a sort of "common currency" that assist modules and programmes to be more transparent at both local level and at an international level. The many advantages of learning outcomes will be discussed in more detail in Chapter 5.

2.4 Learning outcomes and competences

In some papers in the literature, the term "competence" is used in association with learning outcomes. It is difficult to find a precise definition for the term competence. Adam (2004) comments that "some take a narrow view and associate competence just with skills acquired by training". A project entitled *Tuning Educational Structures in Europe* was initiated in 2000 (Tuning Project, URL 6). In this project, the term competence is used to represent a combination of attributes in terms of knowledge and its application, skills, responsibilities and attitudes and an attempt is made to describe the extent to which a person is capable of performing them. The first two phases of the Tuning Project involved subjects areas like Business Administration, Chemistry, Education Sciences, Earth Science (Geology), History, Mathematics, Physics, European Studies and Nursing.

The lack of clarity in terms of defining the term competence is also apparent in the ECTS Users' Guide (2005), which describes competences as "a dynamic combination of attributes, abilities and attitudes. Fostering these competences is the object of educational programmes. Competences are formed in various course units and assessed at different stages. They may be divided in subject-area related competences (specific to a field of study) and generic competences (common to any degree course)."

Since there does not appear to be a common understanding of the term competence in the literature, learning outcomes have become more commonly used than competences when describing what students are expected to know, understand and/or be able to demonstrate at the end of a module or programme.

Chapter 3
How do I write Learning Outcomes?

In outcome-based education the educational outcomes are clearly and unambiguously specified. These determine the curriculum content and its organisation, the teaching methods and strategies, the courses offered, the assessment process, the educational environment and the curriculum timetable. They also provide a framework for curriculum evaluation.

(Harden et al., 1999a)

3.1 Introduction

The task of writing learning outcomes has been made considerably easier for us due to the work of Benjamin Bloom (1913 – 1999), Fig. 3.1. Bloom studied in Pennsylvania State University and graduated with a bachelor's and master's degree from that institution. Bloom worked with a very famous educationalist called Ralph Tyler at the University of Chicago and graduated with a PhD in Education from that university in 1942.

Fig. 3.1 Benjamin Bloom (1913 - 1999).

Bloom was a gifted teacher and was particularly interested in the thought processes of students when they were interacting with what was being taught. He carried out research in the development of classification of levels of thinking during the learning process. He believed that learning was a process and that our job as teachers was to design lessons and tasks to help students to meet the objectives that have been set. Bloom's most famous contribution to education was that he drew up levels of these thinking behaviours from the simple recall of facts at the lowest level up to the process of evaluation at the highest level. His publication *Taxonomy of Educational Objectives: Handbook 1, the Cognitive Domain* (Bloom et al., 1956) has become widely used throughout the world to assist in the preparation of evaluation materials. (The term *taxonomy* implies a classification or categorisation or arrangement.) The taxonomy describes how we build upon our former learning to develop more complex levels of understanding. Many teachers have made great use of Bloom's Taxonomy because of the structure it provides in areas like the assessment of learning. In recent years, attempts have been made to revise Bloom's Taxonomy (Anderson & Krathwohl, 2001; Krathwohl, 2002) but the original works of Bloom and his co-workers are still the most widely quoted in the literature.

Bloom proposed that knowing is composed of six successive levels arranged in a hierarchy as shown in Fig. 3.2.

Fig. 3.2 Bloom proposed that our thinking can be divided into six increasingly complex levels from the simple recall of facts at the lowest level to evaluation at the highest level.

Bloom's taxonomy was not simply a classification scheme – it was an effort by him to arrange the various thinking processes in a hierarchy. In this hierarchy, each level depends on the student's ability to perform at the level or levels that are below it. For example, for a student to apply knowledge (stage 3) he or she would need to have both the necessary information (stage 1) and understanding of this information (stage 2).

When talking about teaching, Bloom always advocated that when teaching and assessing students we should bear in mind that learning is a process and that the teacher should try to get the thought processes of the students to move up into the higher order stages of synthesis and evaluation. This "thinking" area is commonly called the cognitive ("knowing") domain since it involves thought processes.

3.2 Writing learning outcomes in the cognitive domain

Bloom's taxonomy is frequently used for writing learning outcomes as it provides a ready-made structure and list of verbs. These verbs are the key to writing learning outcomes. Bloom's original list of verbs was limited and has been extended by various authors over the years. In this handbook, the list of verbs has been compiled from Bloom's original publication and a study of the more modern literature in this area. It is not claimed that the list of verbs for each stage is an exhaustive list, but it is hoped that the reader will find the lists to be quite comprehensive. A glossary of terms commonly used in this handbook is given in Appendix 1.

Each stage of Bloom's taxonomy is now considered and the corresponding list of verbs relating to each stage is given. Note that since learning outcomes are concerned with what the students can **do** at the end of the learning activity, all of these verbs are active (action) verbs.

3.2.1 Knowledge

Knowledge may be defined as the ability to recall or remember facts without necessarily understanding them. Some of the active verbs used to assess knowledge are shown in Fig. 3.3.

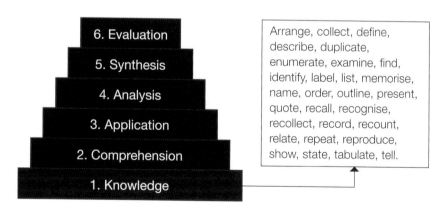

Fig. 3.3 Some active verbs used to test knowledge

Some examples of learning outcomes that demonstrate evidence
of knowledge are:

- Recall genetics terminology: homozygous, heterozygous, phenotype, genotype, homologous chromosome pair, etc.
- Identify and consider ethical implications of scientific investigations.
- Describe how and why laws change and the consequences of such changes on society.
- List the criteria to be taken into account when caring for a patient with tuberculosis.
- Define what behaviours constitute unprofessional practice in the solicitor - client relationship.
- Describe the processes used in engineering when preparing a design brief for a client.

Note that each learning outcome begins with an action verb.

3.2.2 Comprehension

Comprehension may be defined as the ability to understand and interpret learned information. Some of the action verbs used to assess comprehension are shown in Fig. 3.4.

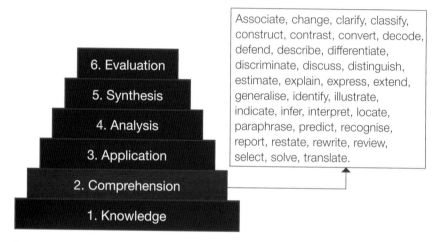

Fig. 3.4 Some action verbs used to assess comprehension

Some examples of learning outcomes that demonstrate evidence of comprehension are:

- Differentiate between civil and criminal law.
- Identify participants and goals in the development of electronic commerce.
- Predict the genotype of cells that undergo meiosis and mitosis.
- Explain the social, economic and political effects of World War I on the post-war world.
- Classify reactions as exothermic and endothermic.
- Recognise the forces discouraging the growth of the educational system in Ireland in the 19th century.

3.2.3 Application

Application may be defined as the ability to use learned material in new situations, e.g. put ideas and concepts to work in solving problems. Some of the action verbs used to assess application are shown in Fig. 3.5.

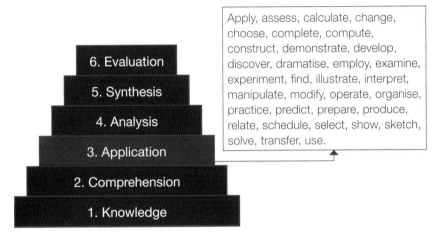

Apply, assess, calculate, change, choose, complete, compute, construct, demonstrate, develop, discover, dramatise, employ, examine, experiment, find, illustrate, interpret, manipulate, modify, operate, organise, practice, predict, prepare, produce, relate, schedule, select, show, sketch, solve, transfer, use.

6. Evaluation

5. Synthesis

4. Analysis

3. Application

2. Comprehension

1. Knowledge

Fig. 3.5 Some active verbs used to assess application. Some examples of learning outcomes that demonstrate evidence of application are:

- Construct a timeline of significant events in the history of Australia in the 19th century.

- Apply knowledge of infection control in the maintenance of patient care facilities.

- Select and employ sophisticated techniques for analysing the efficiencies of energy usage in complex industrial processes.

- Relate energy changes to bond breaking and formation.

- Modify guidelines in a case study of a small manufacturing firm to enable tighter quality control of production.

- Show how changes in the criminal law affected levels of incarceration in Scotland in the 19th century.

- Apply principles of evidence-based medicine to determine clinical diagnoses.

3.2.4 Analysis

Analysis may be defined as the ability to break down information into its components, e.g. look for inter-relationships and ideas (understanding of organisational structure). Some of the action verbs used to assess analysis are shown in Fig. 3.6.

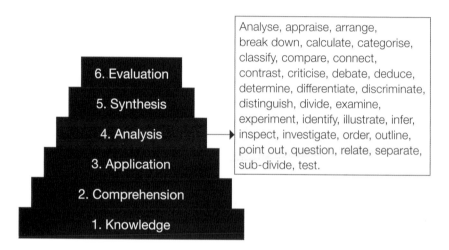

Fig. 3.6 Some active verbs used to assess analysis

Some examples of learning outcomes that demonstrate evidence of analysis are:

- Analyse why society criminalises certain behaviours.
- Compare and contrast the different electronic business models.
- Debate the economic and environmental effects of energy conversion processes.
- Compare the classroom practice of a newly qualified teacher with that of a teacher of 20 years teaching experience.
- Calculate gradient from maps in m, km, % and ratio.

3.2.5 Synthesis

Synthesis may be defined as the ability to put parts together. Some of the active verbs used to assess synthesis are shown in Fig. 3.7.

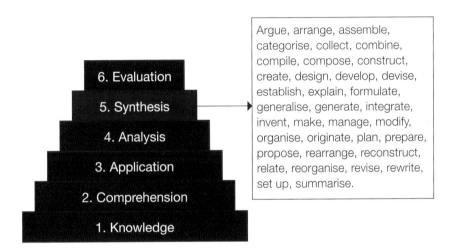

Fig. 3.7 Some active verbs used to assess synthesis

Some examples of learning outcomes that demonstrate evidence of synthesis are:

- Recognise and formulate problems that are amenable to energy management solutions.
- Propose solutions to complex energy management problems both verbally and in writing.
- Summarise the causes and effects of the 1917 Russian revolutions.
- Relate the sign of enthalpy changes to exothermic and endothermic reactions.
- Organise a patient education programme.

3.2.6 Evaluation

Evaluation may be defined as the ability to judge the value of material for a given purpose. Some of the action verbs used to assess evaluation are shown in Fig. 3.8.

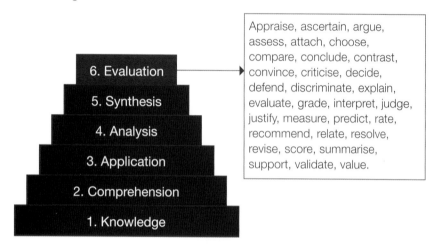

Appraise, ascertain, argue, assess, attach, choose, compare, conclude, contrast, convince, criticise, decide, defend, discriminate, explain, evaluate, grade, interpret, judge, justify, measure, predict, rate, recommend, relate, resolve, revise, score, summarise, support, validate, value.

6. Evaluation
5. Synthesis
4. Analysis
3. Application
2. Comprehension
1. Knowledge

Fig. 3.8 Some active verbs used to assess evaluation

Some examples of learning outcomes that demonstrate evidence of evaluation are:

- Assess the importance of key participants in bringing about change in Irish history.

- Evaluate marketing strategies for different electronic business models.

- Summarise the main contributions of Michael Faraday to the field of electromagnetic induction.

- Predict the effect of change of temperature on the position of equilibrium.

- Evaluate the key areas contributing to the craft knowledge of experienced teachers.

Note that the verbs used in the above six categories are not exclusive to any one particular category. Some verbs appear in more than one category. For example, a mathematical calculation may involve merely applying a given formula (application – stage 3) or it may involve analysis (stage 4) as well as application.

3.3 Writing learning outcomes in the affective domain

Whilst the cognitive domain is the most widely used of Bloom's Taxonomy, Bloom and his co-workers also carried out research on the **affective** ("attitudes", "feelings", "values") domain (Bloom et al., 1964). This domain is concerned with issues relating to the emotional component of learning and ranges from basic willingness to receive information to the integration of beliefs, ideas and attitudes. In order to describe the way in which we deal with things emotionally, Bloom and his colleagues developed five major categories:

1. **Receiving:** This refers to a willingness to receive information, e.g. the individual accepts the need for a commitment to service, listens to others with respect, shows sensitivity to social problems, etc.

2. **Responding:** This refers to the individual actively participating in his or her own learning, e.g. shows interest in the subject, is willing to give a presentation, participates in class discussions, enjoys helping others, etc.

3. **Valuing:** This ranges from simple acceptance of a value to one of commitment, e.g. the individual demonstrates belief in democratic processes, appreciates the role of science in our everyday lives, shows concern for the welfare of others, shows sensitivity towards individual and cultural differences, etc.

4. **Organisation:** This refers to the process that individuals go through as they bring together different values, resolve conflicts among them and start to internalise the values, e.g. recognises the need for balance between freedom and responsibility in a democracy, accepts responsibility for his or her own behaviour, accepts professional ethical standards, adapts behaviour to a value system, etc.

5. **Characterisation:** At this level the individual has a value system in terms of his/her beliefs, ideas and attitudes that control their behaviour in a consistent and predictable manner, e.g. displays self reliance in working independently, displays a professional commitment to ethical practice, shows good personal, social and emotional adjustment, maintains good health habits, etc.

The major categories of the affective domain and some active verbs commonly used when writing learning outcomes for this domain are shown in Fig. 3.9.

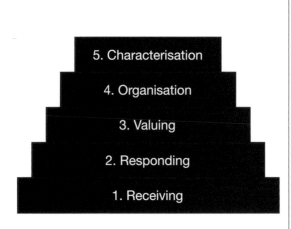

Act, adhere, appreciate, ask, accept, answer, assist, attempt, challenge, combine, complete, conform, co-operate, defend, demonstrate (a belief in), differentiates, discuss, display, dispute, embrace, follow, hold, initiate, integrate, justify, listen, order, organise, participate, practice, join, share, judge, praise, question, relate, report, resolve, share, support, synthesise, value.

Fig. 3.9 The affective domain and some active verbs used in writing learning outcomes in the affective domain

Bloom and his colleagues and subsequent authors have linked the various levels in the affective domain to specific verbs. However, this level of detail is not required in the present context.

Some examples of learning outcomes in the affective domain are:

- Accept the need for professional ethical standards.
- Appreciate the need for confidentiality in the professional client relationship.
- Value a willingness to work independently.
- Relate well to students of all abilities in the classroom.
- Appreciate the management challenges associated with high levels of change in the public sector.
- Display a willingness to communicate well with patients.
- Resolve conflicting issues between personal beliefs and ethical considerations.
- Participate in class discussions with colleagues and with teachers.
- Embrace a responsibility for the welfare of children taken into care.
- Display a professional commitment to ethical practice.

3.4 Writing learning outcomes in the psychomotor domain

The psychomotor domain mainly emphasises physical skills involving co-ordination of the brain and muscular activity. From a study of the literature, it is true to say that this domain has been less well discussed in the field of education than either the cognitive or affective domain. The psychomotor domain is commonly used in areas like laboratory science subjects, health sciences, art, music, engineering, drama and physical education. Bloom and his research team did not complete detailed work on the psychomotor domain as they claimed lack of experience in teaching these skills. However, a number of authors have suggested various versions of taxonomies to describe the development of skills and co-ordination.

For example, Dave (1970) proposed a hierarchy consisting of five levels:

1. **Imitation:** Observing the behaviour of another person and copying this behaviour. This is the first stage in learning a complex skill.

2. **Manipulation:** Ability to perform certain actions by following instructions and practising skills.

3. **Precision:** At this level, the student has the ability to carry out a task with few errors and become more precise without the presence of the original source. The skill has been attained and proficiency is indicated by smooth and accurate performance.

4. **Articulation:** Ability to co-ordinate a series of actions by combining two or more skills. Patterns can be modified to fit special requirements or solve a problem.

5. **Naturalisation:** Displays a high level of performance naturally ("without thinking"). Skills are combined, sequenced and performed consistently with ease.

This hierarchy and some examples of action verbs for writing learning outcomes in the psychomotor domain are shown in Fig. 3.10.

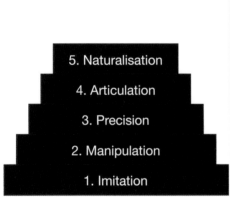

Adapt, adjust, administer, alter, arrange, assemble, balance, bend, build, calibrate, choreograph, combine, construct, copy, design, deliver, detect, demonstrate, differentiate (by touch), dismantle, display, dissect, drive, estimate, examine, execute, fix, grasp, grind, handle, heat, manipulate, identify, measure, mend, mime, mimic, mix, operate, organise, perform (skilfully), present, record, refine, sketch, react, use.

5. Naturalisation
4. Articulation
3. Precision
2. Manipulation
1. Imitation

Fig. 3.10 Taxonomy developed for the psychomotor domain (Dave, 1970) and some action verbs used in writing learning outcomes in the psychomotor domain.

Subsequently, Simpson (1972) developed a more detailed hierarchy consisting of seven levels:

1. **Perception:** The ability to use observed cues to guide physical activity.

2. **Set (mindset):** The readiness to take a particular course of action. This can involve mental, physical and emotional disposition.

3. **Guided response:** The trial-and-error attempts at acquiring a physical skill. With practice, this leads to better performance.

4. **Mechanism:** The intermediate stage in learning a physical skill. Learned responses become more habitual and movements can be performed with some confidence and level of proficiency.

5. **Complex Overt Responses:** Physical activities involving complex movement patterns are possible. Responses are automatic and proficiency is indicated by accurate and highly coordinated performance with a minimum of wasted effort.

6. **Adaptation:** At this level, skills are well developed and the individual can modify movements to deal with problem situations or to fit special requirements.

7. **Origination:** The skills are so highly developed that creativity for special situations is possible.

Other taxonomies in the psychomotor domain have been developed by Harrow (1972) and Dawson (1998). Ferris and Aziz (2005) developed a taxonomy in the psychomotor domain specifically for engineering students.

In general, all of the various taxonomies in the psychomotor domain describe a progression from simple observation to mastery of physical skills.

Some authors have linked specific words to particular levels in the hierarchy. However, this level of detail is outside the scope of this handbook.

Some examples of learning outcomes in the psychomotor domain are:

- Deliver effective local anaesthesia in the mandible and maxilla and identify the appropriate agents that may be used.

- Perform at least ten local anaesthetic administrations and evaluate your performance with your instructor.

- Prescribe and process at least ten radiographs and evaluate them with your instructor.

- Demonstrate proficiency in Cardio-Pulmonary Resuscitation.

- Use a range of physiology equipment to measure physiological function.

- Operate the range of instrumentation specified in the module safely and efficiently in the chemistry laboratory.

- Administer successfully and in a safe manner with minimal risk to patient and operator, infiltration and regional nerve block anaesthesia.

- Present the methodology and findings of the research project in an oral report.

- Design a well-illustrated poster presentation to summarise the research project.

- Examine a patient extra-orally and intra-orally.

- Use the following software effectively and skilfully: MS Word, Excel and Powerpoint.

- Perform a surgical dressing using an aseptic technique.

- Sketch the pump characteristic curve, pipeline curve, the pump-pipeline operating point and show how each of these can be altered in a practical manner.

- Record an accurate impression of the mouth and identify all anatomical features of importance.

3.5 General guidelines for writing learning outcomes

There is a great deal of information in the literature on what is considered best practice when writing learning outcomes (Bingham, 1999; Fry et al., 2000; Jenkins and Unwin, 2001; Moon, 2002). In general, when writing learning outcomes, it is helpful to focus on what you expect students to be able to do or demonstrate at the end of the module or programme. It is important that learning outcomes are expressed in simple and unambiguous terms so that they are clearly understood by students, teachers, colleagues, employers and external examiners.

In general, learning outcomes specify the **essential** learning for a module. Therefore, when writing learning outcomes for a module, it is generally agreed that one should specify the minimum acceptable standard to enable a student to pass the module. As a result, it is recommended that you have a small number of important learning outcomes rather than a large number of superficial ones . There is good advice in the literature regarding the number of learning outcomes that should be written for a module. For example, Moon (2002) suggests that "it is unlikely that there will be more than eight learning outcomes per module. If there are more than ten, they are probably specifying too much curricular detail and may then be unmanageable in the process of assessment".
The Educational and Staff Development Unit of the University of Central England, UK states that "we recommend that you aim for between four and eight learning outcomes for each of your modules…" (URL 7). Bingham (1999) recommends that "most units have between five and nine learning outcomes". Clearly, the number of learning outcomes is also dependent on the size of the module. McLean and Looker (2006) recommend that "learning outcomes should be few enough and significant enough to be memorable and meaningful – most courses might aim for five to ten outcomes". In short, a module with about six well-written learning outcomes is ideal but if you find yourself having written more than nine learning outcomes, you have gone too far!

One of the most important points stressed in the literature is that learning outcomes must not simply be a "wish list" of what a student is capable of doing on completion of the learning activity. Learning outcomes must be simply and clearly described and must be capable of being validly assessed.
(The link between learning outcomes and teaching and assessment is discussed in Chapter 5.)

As already discussed, Bloom's Taxonomy (Bloom, 1956) is one of the most useful aids to writing good learning outcomes. The taxonomy provides a ready-made list of verbs and hence is a useful "toolkit" that provides the vocabulary for writing learning outcomes. There is good agreement in the literature regarding the recommendation that when writing learning outcomes, the emphasis must be on active verbs and that certain terms should be avoided:

> *The key word is DO and the key need in drafting learning outcomes is to use active verbs.*
>
> (Jenkins and Unwin, 2001; Fry et al., 2000)

> *Try to avoid ambiguous verbs such as "understand", "know", "be aware" and "appreciate".*
>
> (Bingham J., 1999)

> *Concrete verbs such as "define", "apply" or "analyse" are more helpful for assessment than verbs such as "be exposed to", "understand", "know" "be familiar with".*
>
> (Osters and Tiu, 2003)

> *Vague verbs such as "know" or "understand" are not easily measurable. Substitute, "identify", "define", "describe" or "demonstrate".*
>
> (British Columbia Institute of Technology, 1996)

> *Care should be taken in using words such as 'understand' and 'know' if you cannot be sure that students will understand what it means to know or understand in a given context.*
>
> (McLean and Looker, 2006)

Verbs relating to knowledge outcomes – "know", "understand", "appreciate" – tend to be rather vague, or to focus on the process students have gone through rather than the final outcome of that process, so use action verbs – "solve", evaluate, analyse – to indicate how students can demonstrate acquisition of that knowledge.
(UCE Educational and Staff Development Unit, URL 7)

Certain verbs are unclear and subject to different interpretations in terms of what action they are specifying. Such verbs call for covert behaviour which cannot be observed or measured. These types of verbs should be avoided: know, become aware of, appreciate, learn, understand, become familiar with.
(American Association of Law Libraries, URL 3.)

Moon (2002) summarises the problems caused by the use of vague terms in writing learning outcomes as follows:

Another common fault in the writing of learning outcomes is that they refer to learning and not the representation of learning. A poorly written learning outcome might say, for example: "At the end of the module, the learner will be expected to know the health and safety practices of laboratory work. (Level 1 chemistry)". We can only tell if the student knows these practices if she is caused to demonstrate her knowledge. She might be asked to write a report, to answer questions, to explain the practices orally and so on".
(Moon, 2002 p. 66)

Fry et al. (2000) when giving practical advice for writing learning outcomes recommend the use of "unambiguous action verbs" and list many examples of verbs from Bloom's Taxonomy. In order to show the differences between the vocabulary used in writing aims and learning outcomes, the authors list some examples of verbs as shown in Table 3.2.

Aims	Outcomes
Know	*Distinguish between*
Understand	*Choose*
Determine	*Assemble*
Appreciate	*Adjust*
Grasp	*Identify*
Become familiar	*Solve, apply, list*

Table 3.2 Examples of verbs used in writing aims and learning outcomes. (Fry et al., 2000 p. 51)

Gosling and Moon (2001) give succinct advice to the reader on writing learning outcomes:

> *Keep learning outcomes simple, normally use only one sentence with one verb in each outcome and avoid unnecessary jargon. Occasionally more than one sentence may be used for clarity.*
>
> (Gosling and Moon, 2001 p. 20)

The following guidelines may be of assistance when writing Learning Outcomes:

- Begin each learning outcome with an active verb, followed by the object of the verb followed by a phrase that gives the context.

- Use only one verb per learning outcome.

- Avoid vague terms like know, understand, learn, be familiar with, be exposed to, be acquainted with, and be aware of. As discussed in Chapter 2, these terms are associated with teaching objectives rather than learning outcomes.

- Avoid complicated sentences. If necessary use more than one sentence to ensure clarity.

- Ensure that the learning outcomes of the module relate to the overall outcomes of the programme

- The learning outcomes must be observable and measurable.

- Ensure that the learning outcomes are capable of being assessed.

- When writing learning outcomes, bear in mind the timescale within which the outcomes are to be achieved. There is always the danger that one can be over ambitious when writing learning outcomes. Ask yourself if it is realistic to achieve the learning outcomes within the time and resources available.

- As you work on writing the learning outcomes, bear in mind how these outcomes will be assessed, i.e. how will you know if the student has achieved these learning outcomes? If the learning outcomes are very broad, they may be difficult to assess effectively. If the learning outcomes are very narrow, the list of learning outcomes may be too long and detailed.

- Before finalising the learning outcomes, ask your colleagues and possibly former students if the learning outcomes make sense to them.

- When writing learning outcomes, try to avoid overloading the list with learning outcomes which are drawn from the bottom of Bloom's Taxonomy (e.g. Knowledge and Comprehension in the cognitive domain). Try to challenge the students to use what they have learned by including some learning outcomes drawn from the higher categories (e.g. Application, Analysis, Synthesis and Evaluation) of Bloom's Taxonomy.

It is standard practice when writing learning outcomes for a module, that the list of learning outcomes is usually preceded by a phrase like "On successful completion of this module, students should be able to:".

An example of learning outcomes written by Dr Edith Allen for UCC module RD3003 is given in Table 3.3.

Table 3.3 Learning outcomes for a module in Restorative Dentistry

On successful completion of this module, students should be able to:

- Examine a patient extra-orally and intra-orally.

- Formulate an appropriate treatment plan based on an understanding of the disease process present and a prediction of the likely success.

- Identify dental caries and restore a tooth to functional form following caries removal.

- Record an accurate impression of the mouth and identify all anatomical features of importance.

- Design a partial denture with appropriate support and retention.

- Administer successfully and in a safe manner with minimal risk to patient and operator, infiltration and regional nerve block anaesthesia.

- Communicate with patients and colleagues in an appropriate manner.

An example of learning outcomes written by Dr Noel Woods for UCC module EC1102 is given in Table 3.4

Table 3.4 Learning outcomes for a module in Economics

On successful completion of this module, students should be able to:

- Recognise the main indicators of stock market timing.

- Describe and distinguish between the main economic indicators.

- Interpret Irish National Income and Expenditure Accounts.

- Differentiate between monetary and fiscal policy.

- Perform economic calculations, which enable the learner to appreciate economic concepts with greater clarity.

- Criticise budgetary decisions using economic criteria.

- Construct and interpret company accounts and accounting ratios.

- Formulate appropriate budgetary policy in response to changes in the business cycle.

- Assess the stance of government fiscal policy.

Further examples of learning outcomes written for various modules are given in Appendix 2.

The checklist shown in Table 3.5 may be of help to double check that you have written the learning outcomes according to the standard guidelines.

Table 3.5 Checklist for writing learning outcomes

☐ Have I focussed on outcomes not processes, i.e. have I focussed on what the students are able to demonstrate rather than on what I have done in my teaching?

☐ Have I begun each outcome with an active verb?

☐ Have I used only one active verb per learning outcome?

☐ Have I avoided terms like *know*, *understand*, *learn*, *be familiar with*, *be exposed to*, *be acquainted with*, and *be aware of*?

☐ Are my outcomes observable and measurable?

☐ Are my outcomes capable of being assessed?

☐ Have I included learning outcomes across the range of levels of Bloom's Taxonomy?

☐ Do all the outcomes fit within the aims and content of the module?

☐ Have I the recommended number of outcomes (maximum of nine per module)?

☐ Is it realistic to achieve the learning outcomes within the time and resources available?

The example shown in Table 3.6 may help you to see how the **key** learning outcomes were developed for one particular module.

Table 3.6 Example of development of key learning outcomes

Module Title: Dental Surgery – 5th Year Dental Students
Module Code: DS 5001
Learning outcomes written by Dr Eleanor O'Sullivan.

On successful completion of this module students should be able to:

Cognitive

- Recall anatomy and basic physiology of the head and neck.

- Outline aetiology, symptoms, pathology, diagnosis and treatment of oro-facial diseases.

- List the steps involved in patient assessment, including procedures for specific tests.

- Apply this format to record a thorough case history of an unseen patient.

- Summarise relevant information regarding the patient's current complaint/status.

- Arrange appropriate tests.

- Demonstrate the ability to interpret tests and reports.

- Evaluate all available information and knowledge to generate a differential diagnosis.

- Formulate an appropriate treatment plan and justify the proposal giving due consideration to patient expectations and limitations.

Affective

- Manage patients with facial pain and oro-facial disease.

- Differentiate between patients that can/can not be safely treated by a general dentist.

- Develop good communication skills (verbal and non-verbal).

- Master the skills required to obtain informed consent, deal with medico-legal issues and dental phobia; deliver health promotion advice.

- Demonstrate professional behaviour and good clinical governance.

- Display the capacity to value and participate in projects which require teamwork.

- Manage competing demands on time, including self-directed learning & critical appraisal.

Psychomotor

- Prescribe, and process dental radiographs.

- Administer local anaesthetics safely.

- Perform basic dento-alveolar surgical procedures.

- Prescribe appropriate drugs.

- Master skills required to manage intra- and post-operative complications.

- Recognise, evaluate and manage dental emergencies appropriately.

- Recognise and manage medical emergencies appropriately.

From the above draft, key learning outcomes were identified as shown in the following list:

On successful completion of this module, students should be able to:

- Master the skills required to record a thorough case history, deliver health promotion advice and obtain informed consent dealing with medico-legal issues.

- Summarise relevant information regarding the patient's current condition to generate a differential diagnosis.

- Formulate an appropriate treatment plan and justify the proposal giving due consideration to patient expectations and limitations.

- Arrange appropriate tests and demonstrate the ability to interpret tests and reports.

- Administer local anaesthetics safely and perform basic dento-alveolar surgical procedures in a professional manner showing good clinical governance.

- Recognise, evaluate and manage medical and dental emergencies appropriately.

- Differentiate between patients that can/can not be safely treated by a GDP.

- Manage competing demands on time, including self-directed learning & critical appraisal.

- Master the therapeutic and pharmacological management of patients with facial pain and oro-facial disease.

3.6 Programme learning outcomes

As already discussed, learning outcomes must be capable of being assessed, i.e. they should be written in a way that allows testing of whether or not the student has achieved the outcome. The rules for writing learning outcomes for programmes are the same as those for writing learning outcomes for modules. The general guidance in the literature is that there should be 5 – 10 learning outcomes for a programme and that only the minimum number of outcomes considered to be essential be included. In short, programme learning outcomes describe the essential knowledge, skills and attitudes that it is intended that graduates of the programme will be able to demonstrate.

When drawing up learning outcomes for programmes, it is suggested (Moon 2002) that there could be value in writing two types of learning outcome. The first type of learning outcome refers to those learning outcomes that can be assessed during the programme, i.e. within the various modules. The second type of learning outcome may not be assessed at all but gives an indication to employers and other agencies the type of standard of practical performance that graduates of the programme will display at the end of the programme. These "aspirational" or "desirable" learning outcomes indicate what a good quality student would be expected to achieve by the end of the programme. The situation may be summarised as follows:

> *It is important to note that there are clear differences in the nature of programme outcomes and learning outcomes written for modules. Programme outcomes are written for a typical or average student and they may be aspirational. They are not, therefore, directly testable. For example, programme outcomes may evidence areas of learning that are the outcomes of the student's experience of engagement in the programme, on the basis that the whole may be greater than the sum of its parts.*
>
> (Moon 2002 p.142)

When writing the programme learning outcomes, it is recommended that one should not simply compile all of the learning outcomes from all of the modules in a programme. A programme may be more than simply the sum of the various component modules. For example, there may be some overarching programme learning outcomes, e.g. formulate hypotheses, analyse data and draw conclusions. In addition, you may wish to include some aspirational learning outcomes as discussed above. In addition, where there is a choice of modules within a programme, there may be skills common to all students despite the fact that they may have taken various combinations of modules (Dillon and Hodgkinson, 2000).

When writing programme learning outcomes, it is common practice to use an initial statement like "On completion of this programme, it is expected that the students will be able to…"

This statement is followed by the list of learning outcomes written according to the guidelines already discussed for module learning outcomes. For example, some of the Programme Learning Outcomes for a Master's degree in Computer Science (URL 8) are listed in Table 3.7.

Table 3.7 Example of programme learning outcomes for a postgraduate computer science degree

On completion of this programme, it is expected that the students will be able to:

- Perform problem solving in academic and industrial environments.

- Use, manipulate and create large computational systems.

- Work effectively as a team member.

- Organise and pursue a scientific or industrial research project.

- Write theses and reports to a professional standard, equivalent in presentational qualities to that of publishable papers.

- Prepare and present seminars to a professional standard.

- Perform independent and efficient time management.

- Use a full range of IT skills and display a mature computer literacy.

A further example of some of the programme learning outcomes (URL 9) listed for an engineering degree are shown in Table 3.8.

Table 3.8 Example of programme learning outcomes for an undergraduate engineering degree

On completion of this programme, it is expected that students will be able to:

- Derive and apply solutions from knowledge of sciences, engineering sciences, technology and mathematics.

- Identify, formulate, analyse and solve engineering problems.

- Design a system, component or process to meet specified needs and to design and conduct experiments to analyse and interpret data.

- Work effectively as an individual, in teams and in multi-disciplinary settings together with the capacity to undertake lifelong learning.

- Communicate effectively with the engineering community and with society at large.

Some authors recommend the use of course mapping to help to get an overview of how the programme learning outcomes are covered within the various courses offered in the programme (URL 10). The coverage of each programme learning outcomes within the courses may be shown in the form of a grid. Fig. 3.11.

Fig. 3.11 Map of programme learning outcomes and courses within programmes

Programme Learning Outcome	Course 1	Course 1	Course 3	Course 4
Outcome 1	×		×	
Outcome 2		×		×
Outcome 3	×		×	
Outcome 4	×			
Outcome 5				×
Outcome 6		×	×	×

When writing learning outcomes for programmes, it is important to ensure that, where applicable, the learning outcomes for professional bodies are incorporated into the programme outcomes.

Further examples of programme learning outcomes in a wide variety of subject areas are given in URL 11.

Chapter 4
How are Learning Outcomes linked to Teaching and Assessment?

If students are to learn desired outcomes in a reasonably effective manner, then the teacher's fundamental task is to get students to engage in learning activities that are likely to result in their achieving those outcomes… what the student does in determining what is learned is more important than what the teacher does.

(Shuell, 1986)

4.1 Introduction

We have seen in Section 3.5 that, when writing learning outcomes, it is important to write them in such a way that they are capable of being assessed. Moon (2002) clearly emphasises this point when discussing the importance of writing learning outcomes that can be assessed:

> *Certainly, all learning outcomes should be assessable; in other words, they should be written in terms that enable testing of whether or not the student has achieved the outcome.*
>
> (Moon, 2002 p.75)

Clearly, it is necessary to have some form of assessment tool or technique in order to determine the extent to which learning outcomes have been achieved. Examples of direct assessment techniques are the use of written examinations, project work, portfolios, grading system with rubrics, theses, reflective journals, performance assessment, etc. Examples of indirect assessment methods are surveys of employers, comparison with peer institutions, surveys of past graduates, retention rates, analyses of curricula, etc.

The challenge for teachers is to ensure that there is alignment between teaching methods, assessment techniques, assessment criteria and learning outcomes. This connection between teaching, assessment and learning outcomes helps to make the overall learning experience more transparent and meaningful for students. Ramsden (2003) points out that evidence collected from student course evaluations shows that clear expectations on the part of students of what is required of them are a vitally important part of students' effective learning. Lack of clarity in this area is almost always associated with negative evaluations, learning difficulties, and poor student performance. Toohey (1999) recommends that the best way to help students understand how they must achieve learning outcomes is by clearly setting out the assessment techniques and the assessment criteria.

In terms of teaching and learning, there is a dynamic equilibrium between teaching strategies on one side and learning outcomes and assessment on the other.

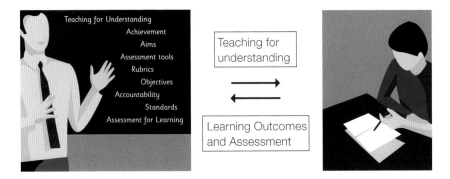

It is important that the assessment tasks mirror the learning outcomes since, as far as the students are concerned, the assessment **is** the curriculum: "From our students' point of view, assessment always defines the actual curriculum" (Ramsden, 2003). This situation is represented graphically by Biggs (2003b) as shown in Fig. 4.1.

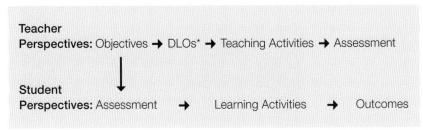

* Desired Learning Outcomes

Fig. 4.1 Different representations of teacher and student perspectives (Biggs, 2003)

In stressing this point, Biggs (2003) emphasises the strong link between the curriculum and assessment as follows:

> *To the teacher, assessment is at the end of the teaching-learning sequence of events, but to the student it is at the beginning. If the curriculum is reflected in the assessment, as indicated by the downward arrow, the teaching activities of the teacher and the learner activities of the learner are both directed towards the same goal. In preparing for the assessment, students will be learning the curriculum.*

(Biggs 2003)

One cannot over-emphasise the importance of assessment in the teaching and learning process. As already stated (Ramsden, 2003) as far as the students are concerned, the assessment **is** the curriculum. They will learn what they think they will be assessed on, not what may be on the curriculum or even what has been covered in lectures! The old adage that "assessment is the tail that wags the dog" is very true.

Since assessment is a driving force for learning, we must be clear in our minds about the type of learning we want from our students so that the assessment tasks we set them will help achieve the desired learning. A flowchart similar to that shown in Fig. 4.2 may be of help in clarifying the steps involved in the development, refining and assessment of learning outcomes.

Fig 4.2 Flowchart summarising the steps involved in the development and refining of learning outcomes and their assessment

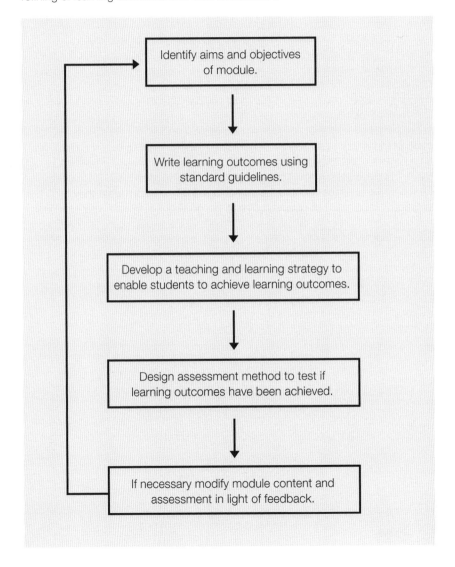

4.2 Linking learning outcomes, teaching and assessment

Assessment is often described in terms of **formative assessment** or **summative assessment.** Formative assessment has been described as being assessment **for** learning. It has been described as assessment that "refers to all those activities undertaken by teachers, and by the students in assessing themselves, which provide information to be used as feedback to modify the teaching and learning activities in which they are engaged" (Black and Williams, 1998). In other words, formative assessment helps to inform the teacher and the students as to how the students are progressing. Formative assessment is usually carried out at the beginning of a programme or during a programme. The students' performances on the assessment tasks can help the teacher to make decisions about the direction of the teaching to help the learning process. It has been clearly shown (Black and Williams, 1998) that by giving feedback to students, formative assessment can help improve the learning and performance of students.

The feedback that the students receive from the teacher helps to improve their learning. For example, formative assessment can include course work where the student receives feedback that will be of help in improving the next performance. It can also include discussions between a mentor and a student where areas for attention are identified (Brown and Knight, 1994).

The main characteristics of formative assessment include:

- Identification by teachers and students of the learning outcomes and the criteria for achieving these;
- The provision of clear and rich feedback in an effective and timely fashion;
- The active involvement of students in their own learning;
- Good communication between teacher and students;
- The response by the teacher to the needs of the students.

An example of formative assessment could be asking the students to give a presentation to the rest of the class group. This can help to enhance the student's knowledge, research skills, communication skills and organisational skills. Whilst formative assessment may be used as part of continuous assessment, it is not usually included in the final grade awarded to students. Indeed, many educationalists believe that it should not be included. For example, Donnelly and Fitzmaurice argue that "in order for students to have the maximum opportunity to learn in a module, then there must be some option for a formative assessment which does not contribute to the final grade. Students can then obtain feedback which will allow them to address any gaps in their knowledge or skills" (Donnelly and Fitzmaurice, 2005). In short, formative assessment is part of the teaching process rather than the grading process.

Summative assessment is assessment that tries to summarise student learning at some point in time – usually at the end of a module or programme. Summative assessment has been described as "end-of-course assessment and essentially means that this is assessment which produces a measure which sums up someone's achievement and which has no other real use except as a description of what has been achieved" (Brown and Knight, 1994).

Thus, the use of summative assessment enables a grade to be generated that reflects the student's performance. Unfortunately, summative assessment is often restricted to just the traditional examination paper and does not involve other areas like project work, portfolios or essays. Because of the nature of summative assessment, not all learning outcomes can be assessed at any one time. Assessment of just a sample of learning outcomes is common.

In theory, **continuous assessment** is a combination of summative and formative assessment. In practice, continuous assessment often amounts to repeated summative assessments with marks being recorded but little or no specific feedback being given to students.

Biggs (2003a) points out that different assessment tasks are associated with different kinds of learning. These are summarised in Table 4.1.

Table 4.1 Assessment tasks and the different kinds of learning assessed,
Adapted from Biggs (2003a)

Assessment Mode	Most likely kind of learning assessed
Extended prose, essay type	
Essay exam	Rote, question spotting, speed structuring
Open book	As for exam, but less memory, coverage
Assignment, take-home	Read widely, interrelate, organise, apply
Objective test	
Multiple choice	Recognition, strategy, comprehension,
Ordered outcome	Hierarchies of understanding
Performance assessment	
Practicum	Skills needed in real life
Seminar, presentation	Communication skills
Posters	Concentrating on relevance, application
Interviewing	Responding interactively
Critical incidents	Reflection, application, sense of relevance
Project	Application, research skills
Reflective journal	Reflection, application, sense of relevance
Case study, problems	Application, professional skills
Portfolio	Reflection, creativity, unintended outcomes
Rapid assessments (large group)	
Concept maps	Coverage, relationships
Venn diagrams	Relationships
One minute/three-minute paper	Level of understanding, sense of relevance
Short answer	Recall units of information, coverage
Letter to a friend	Holistic understanding, application, reflection
Cloze	Comprehension of main ideas

Clearly, it is important that the method of assessment that we use should attempt to test whether or not the learning outcomes have been achieved. Interestingly, it has been found that the range of assessment of students is very limited with approximately 80% of assessment being in the form of exams, essays and reports of some kind (Brown,1999). For example, in a study of UCD assessment practices (O'Neill, 2002) it was found that a random sample of 83 teaching staff used a total of 256 assessments when asked to describe one of their courses, i.e. approximately 3 assessments per course. Of these assessments, the majority (84%) were summative and the minority (16%) formative.

Developing links between learning outcomes, teaching strategies, student activities and assessment tasks is very challenging for the teacher. Table 4.2 may be of help in developing these links.

Table 4.2 Linking learning outcomes, teaching and learning activities and assessment

Learning outcomes		Teaching and Learning Activities	Assessment
Cognitive ↕	Demonstrate Knowledge Comprehension Application Analysis Synthesis. Evaluation	Lectures Tutorials Discussions Laboratory work Clinical work	End of module exam Multiple choice tests Essays Practical
Affective ↕	Integration of beliefs, ideas and attitudes	Group work Seminar Peer group presentation	assessment Fieldwork Clinical practice Presentation Project work
Psychomotor	Acquisition of physical skills		

It is important to ensure that the method of assessment adequately assesses the learning outcomes. There may not be just one method of assessment to satisfy all learning outcomes and it may be necessary to choose a number of assessment methods.

An example showing the application of the above table to Module ED2100 of the BSc(Ed) programme in UCC is given in Table 4.3 on the facing page.

Table 4.3 Linking learning outcomes, teaching and learning activities and assessment for module ED2100 in BSc(Ed) programme

Learning outcomes	Teaching and Learning Activities	Assessment 10 credit module Mark = 200
Cognitive • *Recognise and apply the basic principles of classroom management and discipline* • *Identify the key characteristics of high quality science teaching* • *Develop a comprehensive portfolio of lesson plans*	*Lectures (12)* *Tutorials (6)* *Observation of classes (6) of experienced science teacher (mentor)*	*End of module exam.* *Portfolio of lesson plans* **(100 marks)**
Affective • *Display a willingness to co-operate with members of teaching staff in their assigned school* • *Participate successfully in Peer Assisted Learning project*	*Participation in mentoring feedback sessions in school (4)* *Participation in 3 sessions of UCC Peer Assisted Learning (PAL) Programme* *Peer group presentation*	*Report from school mentor* *End of project report* **(50 marks)**
Psychomotor • *Demonstrate good classroom presentation skills* • *Perform laboratory practical work in a safe and efficient manner*	*Teaching practice 6 weeks at 2 hours per week* *Laboratory work*	*Supervision of Teaching practice* *Assessment of teaching skills* **(50 marks)**

The above level of detail is not, of course, required in the description of modules in UCC but it can be helpful to set up a table like the above when designing or revising modules.

Biggs (2003) refers to this type of process as involving **constructive alignment.** This means that the curriculum is designed so that the teaching activities, learning activities and assessment tasks are co-ordinated with the learning outcomes. (The *constructive* part refers to the type of learning and what the student does. The *alignment* part refers to what the teacher does). Biggs points out that in a good teaching system, the method of teaching, learning activities and method of assessment are all co-ordinated to support student learning.

> *When there is alignment between what we want, how we teach and how we assess, teaching is likely to be much more effective than when it is not (aligned)... Traditional transmission theories of teaching ignore alignment.*
>
> (Biggs 2003a)

It is clear from the above, that there are three basic areas involved in the constructive alignment of any module:

1. Clearly defining the learning outcomes.

2. Selecting teaching and learning methods that are likely to ensure that the learning outcomes are achieved.

3. Assessing the student learning outcomes and checking to see how well they match with what was intended.

4.3 Assessment criteria and learning outcomes

We have seen in Section 3.5 that learning outcomes specify the minimum acceptable standard to enable a student to pass a module. Student performances above this basic threshold level are differentiated by applying grading criteria. Grading criteria are statements that indicate what a student must demonstrate to achieve higher grades. These statements help to differentiate the levels of performance of a student. By making these criteria clear to students, it is hoped that students will aim for the highest levels of performance.

Giving only a grade to a student does not provide adequate feedback on his/her performance since the grade simply indicates an overall level of competency. This overall grade does not identify strengths and weaknesses on specific learning outcomes. However, if the grading system is tied to some form of scoring guide, it can be a very useful way of identifying areas for improvement that need to be addressed.

A scoring guide that is used in assessment is often referred to as a **rubric**. A rubric is a grading tool used to describe the criteria used in grading the performance of students. In general, each rubric consists of a set of criteria and marks or grades associated with these criteria. Thus, rubrics help to define the criteria of the system of assessment by describing performance at different points on a rating scale.

For example, a scoring rubric used for one of the learning outcomes in module ED6001 of the Master's Degree in Science Education is shown in Table 4.4 on page 68.

For details on developing detailed rubrics, the reader is referred to the website developed by Mullinix of the University of Monmouth (URL 12).

Table 4.4 Linking learning outcomes and assessment criteria

Learning outcome	Assessment criteria				
	Grade 1	Grade 2 : 1	Grade 2 :2	Pass	Fail
On successful completion of this module, students should be able to: • Summarise evidence from the science education literature to support development of a line of argument.	Outstanding use of literature showing excellent ability to synthesise evidence in analytical way to formulate clear conclusions.	Very good use of literature showing high ability to synthesise evidence in analytical way to formulate clear conclusions.	Good use of literature showing good ability to synthesise evidence in analytical way to formulate clear conclusions	Limited use of literature showing fair ability to synthesise evidence to formulate conclusions.	Poor use of literature showing lack of ability to synthesise evidence to formulate conclusions

Chapter 5
Looking towards the future with Learning Outcomes

Much depends on how they (learning outcomes) are constructed and whether (and how) they include knowledge, skills, abilities/attitudes and understanding. Badly constructed, narrow and limiting learning outcomes are not appropriate for higher education where creativity and imaginative leaps are highly valued.

(Adam, 2004)

5.1 Introduction

We saw in Chapter 2 that international trends in education show a shift from the traditional "teacher centred" approach to a more "student centred" approach. While traditionally the focus was on what the teacher did, in recent years the focus has been on what students have learned and can demonstrate at the end of a module or programme. Among the key characteristics of outcome-based education listed by Harden (2002) are:

- The development of clearly defined and published learning outcomes that must be achieved before the end of the programme.

- The design of a curriculum, learning strategies and learning opportunities to ensure the achievement of the learning outcome.

- An assessment process matched to the learning outcomes and the assessment of individual students to ensure that they have achieved the outcomes.

5.2 Advantages of learning outcomes

Whilst there has been some criticism of outcome-based education in the literature, in general, it is true to say that this type of education has received very strong support at an international level. For example, Jenkins and Unwin (2001) assert that learning outcomes:

- Help teachers to tell students more precisely what is expected of them.

- Help students to learn more effectively: students know where they stand and the curriculum is made more open to them.

- Help teachers to design their materials more effectively by acting as a template for them.

- Make it clear what students can hope to gain from following a particular course or lecture.

- Help teachers select the appropriate teaching strategy matched to the intended learning outcome, e.g. lecture, seminar, group work, tutorial, discussion, peer group presentation or laboratory class.

- Help teachers to tell their colleagues more precisely what a particular activity is designed to achieve.

- Assist in setting examinations based on the materials delivered.

- Ensure that appropriate teaching and assessment strategies are employed.

When writing about the embracing of learning outcomes in medical education, Harden (2002a) comments that "where it has been implemented, outcome based education has had a significant and beneficial impact. Clarification of the learning outcomes in medical education helps teachers, wherever they are, to decide what they should teach and assess, and students what they are expected to learn". In another paper, Harden (2002b) describes how learning outcomes have been used to develop a model for use in the medical training:

> *Learning outcomes can be specified in a way that covers the range of necessary competences and emphasises the integration of different competences in the practice of medicine. An important feature of the three-circle model of learning outcomes is that it does just that. In the inner circle are the seven learning outcomes relating to what a doctor is able to do, i.e. the technical competences expected of a doctor ('doing the right thing'); in the middle circle the learning outcomes relating to how the doctor approaches his or her task with knowledge and understanding and appropriate attitude and decision-making strategies ('doing the thing right'); and in the outer circle the ongoing development of the doctor as an individual and as a professional ('the right person doing it').*
> (Harden, 2002b, p.153)

The model described above is shown in Figure 5.1

Figure 5.1 A three-circle model for outcome based education in medicine (Harden 1999b)

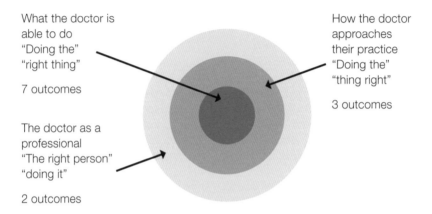

What the doctor is able to do
"Doing the" "right thing"

7 outcomes

How the doctor approaches their practice
"Doing the" "thing right"

3 outcomes

The doctor as a professional
"The right person" "doing it"

2 outcomes

Toohey (1999) agues that learning outcomes are valuable because:

- They clarify the educational purpose and can help in the design of other aspects of the programme. In a constructively aligned course, learning outcomes provide a guide to learning and assessment activities.

- They express the educational purpose of the teacher to students so that students know what the course offers them and what is expected of them. In other words, learning outcomes help students focus on what's important in the course.

- They help the teacher to reconceptualise his or her educational purpose from the student's point of view, i.e. in terms of what the student can be expected to be able to do as a result of completing the module or programme.

Adam (2004) summarises the advantages of learning outcomes under four main headings:

(i) Course and module design

Learning outcomes can:

- Help to ensure consistency of delivery across modules and programmes.
- Aid curriculum design by clarifying areas of overlap between modules and programmes.
- Help course designers to determine precisely the key purposes of a course and to see how components of the syllabus fit and how learning progression is incorporated.
- Highlight the relationship between teaching, learning and assessment and help improve course design and the student experience.
- Promote reflection on assessment and the development of assessment criteria and more effective and varied assessment.

(ii) Quality assurance

Learning outcomes:

- Increase transparency and the comparability of standards between and within qualifications.
- Possess greater credibility and utility than traditional qualifications.
- Play a key role by acting as points of reference for establishing and assessing standards.

(iii) Students

Learning outcomes provide:

- Comprehensive sets of statements of exactly what the students will be able to achieve after successful study.

- Clear information to help students with their choice of module and programme. This can lead to more effective learning.

- Clear information to employers and higher education institutions on the achievements and characteristics associated with particular qualifications.

(iv) Mobility

Learning outcomes:

- Contribute to the mobility of students by facilitating the recognition of their qualifications.

- Improve the transparency of qualifications.

- Simplify credit transfer.

- Provide a common format that helps promote lifelong learning and can assist in creating multiple routes through and between different educations systems.

Finally, the University of Central England Educational and Staff Development Unit points out that learning outcomes can help to avoid plagiarism and gives the following two examples:

- Learning outcome: Students will be able to demonstrate the origins of their ideas by referencing sources used in their work.

- Assessment criterion: Accurate use of the standard referencing styles within the text for all sources used.

5.3 Potential problems with learning outcomes

One of the main concerns about the adoption of learning outcomes is the philosophical one that academic study should be open-ended and that learning outcomes do not fit in with this liberal view of learning (Adam, 2004). This need not be the case if learning outcomes are written according to the standard guidelines. However, if learning outcomes are written within a very narrow framework, this could limit learning and result in a lack of intellectual challenge to students. Other potential problems are:

- There is a danger of an assessment-driven curriculum if learning outcomes are too confined.

- Learning outcomes could give rise to confusion among students and staff if guidelines not adhered to when drawing up these learning outcomes.

5.4 Some concluding points

We have seen that international trends in education show a movement away from the emphasis on a "teacher-centred" approach to a more "outcome-based" approach to education. This movement has gained increased momentum from the Bologna Process with its emphasis on student-centred learning and the need to have more precision and clarity in the design and content of curricula. It is clear that learning outcomes play a key role in ensuring transparency of qualifications and qualification frameworks and also in contributing to the implementation of the various action lines of the Bologna Process throughout the European Higher Education Area.

The requirement to make the teaching and learning process more transparent and more explicit presents a challenge to all of us involved in education. In the short term we must prepare for the immediate challenge of expressing our modules and programmes in terms of learning outcomes. In the longer term, the adoption of the learning outcomes approach has the potential to help us to embrace a more systematic approach to the design of programmes and modules. It is hoped that this handbook will help us all to rise to the challenges posed by the Bologna Process and help us to integrate learning outcomes into our teaching activities, learning activities and assessment tasks.
Bhail ó Dhia ar an obair!

Appendix 1: Glossary of common terms

Account for: Clarify, explain, give reasons for a statement.

Aim: The aim of a module or programme is a broad general statement of teaching intention, i.e. it indicates what the teacher intends to cover in a block of learning.

Analysis: The ability to break down information into its components, e.g. look for inter-relationships and ideas (Bloom's Taxonomy).

Application: The ability to use learned material in new situations, e.g. put ideas and concepts to work in solving problems (Bloom's Taxonomy).

Assess: Evaluate, weigh up.

Assessment: The total range of written, oral and practical tests, examinations, projects and portfolios that are used to evaluate a student's progress in the unit or module of the programme.

Assessment criteria: Descriptions of what a student is expected to do in order to demonstrate that a learning outcome has been achieved.

Bologna Process: The attempt to create the European Higher Education Area by harmonising academic degree standards and quality assurance standards throughout Europe.

Compare: Look for similarities between two areas.

Competences: "Competences represent a dynamic combination of attributes, abilities and attitudes. Fostering these competences is the object of educational programmes. Competences are formed in various course units and assessed at different stages. They may be divided in subject-area related competences (specific to a field of study) and generic competences (common to any degree course)" ECTS Users' Guide (2005).

Comprehension: The ability to understand and interpret learned information (Bloom's Taxonomy).

Constructive alignment: The designing of a curriculum so that the teaching activities, learning activities and assessment tasks are co-ordinated with the learning outcomes.

Continuous assessment: Assessment that takes place within the normal teaching period and contributes to the final assessment.

Contrast: Look for differences between two areas.

Compare and contrast: Look for some points in common between two areas and show where or how they differ.

Coursework: The tasks that are required by a module or unit of a programme.

Credit: The unit used in the European Credit Transfer System (ECTS). ECTS credits are used to measure student workload in terms of time.

Credit accumulation: The system where a specified number of credits must be obtained in order to complete successfully a programme.

Criticise: Using evidence or reasoning, make a judgment about the merits of an argument or theory or opinion.

Define: state the exact meaning of a word or phrase.

Describe: Give a detailed account of a topic.

Diploma Supplement: An annex to the official qualification and is issued in a standard international format. It provides a description of the nature, level, context, content and status of the studies that were pursued and successfully completed by the holder of the qualification.

Discuss: Explain and give various sides of an issue and any implications.

Distinguish (differentiate): look for the difference between.

Evaluation: The ability to judge the value of material for a given purpose (Bloom's Taxonomy).

Examine: Look in detail at a particular area.

Explain: Give details about a point or area of discussion.

Formative assessment: A type of assessment that helps to inform the teacher and the students as to how the students are progressing. Formative assessment is usually carried out at the beginning of or during a programme. The intention is that the feedback that the students receive from the teacher helps to improve their learning.

Grading criteria: Indications of what a student must demonstrate to achieve a higher grade above the minimum requirement to pass a module.

Identify: Recognise and state the existence of a point of argument or concept.

Illustrate: With the aid of examples, clarify a particular area of discussion.

Justify: Explain the grounds for making decisions or drawing conclusions. Formulate answers to the main objections likely to be made.

Knowledge: The ability to recall or remember facts without necessarily understanding them (Bloom's Taxonomy).

Learning outcomes: Statements of what a learner is expected to know, understand and/or be able to demonstrate after completion of a process of learning.

Module: A self-contained fraction of a student's programme workload for the year with a unique examination and a clear set of learning outcomes and appropriate assessment criteria.

Objective: The objective of a module or programme is a specific statement of teaching intention, i.e. it indicates one of the specific areas that the teacher intends to cover in a block of learning.

Outline: Give the main features or general principles of a topic, leaving out minor details and emphasising the structure and arrangement of the topic.

Process: A series of actions, changes or functions that bring about a result.

Rubric: A rubric is a grading tool used to describe the criteria used in grading the performance of students. Thus, a rubric provides a clear guide as to how students' work will be assessed. In general, each rubric consists of a set of criteria and marks or grades associated with these criteria.

State: Present in a brief, clear form without any explanation being needed.

Summarise: Present a concise, clear explanation or account of the area. Give the main points and leave out minor details. (Similar to outline above.)

Summative assessment: Assessment that tries to summarise student learning at some point in time – usually the end of a module or course. The use of summative assessment enables a grade to be generated that reflects the student's performance.

Synthesis: The ability to put parts together (Bloom's Taxonomy).

Taxonomy: A classification based on certain criteria.

Appendix 2: Examples of learning outcomes from UCC modules

(Modules are arranged in alphabetical order according to module code.)

Module Title: Systems Biology
Module Code: BL6005
Learning outcomes written by Dr Siobhán O'Sullivan

On successful completion of this module students should be able to:

- Define the characteristics of cancer cells.

- Distinguish between a proto-oncogene and an oncogene using an example of each, and illustrate the role they both play in the development of cancer.

- Illustrate the cell cycle and differentiate the different stages which occur throughout.

- Compare the lac and trp operons in terms of function and regulation.

- Discuss the importance of gene regulation in bacterial systems using appropriate examples.

Module Title: Team Software Project
Module Code: CS3305
Learning outcomes written by Professor John Morrison

On successful completion of this module students should be able to:

- Define a Project Management Plan.

- Tabulate Testing Plans.

- Contrast alternative implementation procedures.

- Discuss contingency plans.

- Construct working code and test implemented code.

- Schedule tasks to achieve goals.

- Design computer-human interfaces.

- Assess project outcomes with respect to initial stated requirements.

- Differentiate between good and bad computer-human interfaces in terms of the physical interactions and ergonomics required by the program user to achieve the desired result.

Module Title: DS4004
Module Code: Introduction to Dental Surgery
Learning outcomes written by Dr Christine McCreary

On successful completion of this module, students should be able to:

- Obtain and record accurate and comprehensive medical/dental and social histories from patients exercising judgement in relation to the questions and demonstrating empathy and communication skills with the patient.

- Interpret the significance of the history and develop appropriate treatment plans and differential diagnoses, being cognisant of patients' needs and wishes.

- Deliver effective local anaesthesia in the mandible and maxilla and identify the appropriate agents that may be used.

- Perform at least 10 local anaesthetic administrations.

- Identify the appropriate armamentarium and techniques for simple extractions in the maxilla and mandible.

- Perform at least 10 extractions.

- Summarise the different intra oral radiographic techniques employed in general dental practice. Take at least 10 radiographs and evaluate them with your instructor.

- Demonstrate proficiency in CPR (cardiopulmonary resuscitation).

Module Title: Dental Surgery – 5th Year Dental Students
Module Code: DS5001
Learning outcomes written by Dr Eleanor O'Sullivan

On successful completion of this module, students should be able to:

- Master the skills required to record a thorough case history, deliver health promotion advice and obtain informed consent dealing with medico-legal issues.

- Summarise relevant information regarding the patient's current condition to generate a differential diagnosis.

- Formulate an appropriate treatment plan and justify the proposal giving due consideration to patient expectations and limitations.

- Arrange appropriate tests and demonstrate the ability to interpret tests and reports.

- Administer local anaesthetics safely and perform basic dento-alveolar surgical procedures in a Professional manner showing good clinical governance.

- Recognise, evaluate and manage medical and dental emergencies appropriately.

- Differentiate between patients that can/can not be safely treated by a GDP.

- Manage competing demands on time, including self-directed learning & critical appraisal.

- Master the therapeutic and pharmacological management of patients with facial pain and oro-facial disease.

Module Title: Introducing Economics
Module Code: EC1102
Learning outcomes written by Dr Noel Woods

On successful completion of this module, students should be able to:

- Recognise the main indicators of stock market timing.

- Describe and distinguish between the main economic indicators.

- Interpret Irish National Income and Expenditure Accounts.

- Differentiate between monetary and fiscal policy.

- Perform economic calculations, which enable the learner to appreciate economic concepts with greater clarity.

- Criticise budgetary decisions using economic criteria.

- Construct and interpret company accounts and accounting ratios.

- Formulate appropriate budgetary policy in response to changes in the business cycle.

- Assess the stance of government fiscal policy.

Module Title: History of Irish Education
Module Code: ED401
Learning outcomes written by Dr Tracey Connolly

On successful completion of this module students should be able to:

- Describe the Irish Education system and its evolution.

- Discuss enduring features of education in the period studied.

- Apply the skills of a historian in analysing the past.

- Analyse how different administrations approached education.

- Propose approaches that could have been made to the development of education in the context of the time.

- Recognise the problems that confronted the evolution of Irish education.

- Summarise the causes and effects of specific developments in the history of Irish education.

Module Title: General Practice
Module Code: GP4001
Learning outcomes written by Professor Colin Bradley

On successful completion of this module students should be able to:

- Develop a rapport with patients such that they are at ease in discussing their health problem(s).

- Gather appropriate information on the patient's health problem(s) including information on the patient's own perspective on the problem(s).

- Generate a reasonable range of diagnostic possibilities for undifferentiated medical problems presented by patients.

- Investigate these diagnostic possibilities using appropriately focused history taking and selective physical examination.

- Construct a general model for the safe and effective management of patients with multiple and long term health problems.

- Adapt this model to the long term health problems commonly encountered by doctors.

- Construct an appropriate and feasible management plan to deal with the physical, psychological and social aspects of patient's problem(s).

- Negotiate this plan with the patient.

Module Title: Politics of the European Union
Module Code: GV1202
Learning outcomes written by: Dr Mary C. Murphy, Department of Government,
University College Cork

On successful completion of this module students should be able to:

- Explain the logic for the creation of the European Union

- Describe the difference between supra-nationalism and intergovernmentalism.

- Criticise the structure and operation of key EU institutions.

- Evaluate the political and economic impact of selected EU policies.

- Predict the future shape and nature of the EU.

- List the advantages and disadvantages of Irish membership of the EU

- Research and present information effectively and comprehensively.

- Question the meaning of and motivation for political developments generally.

- Analyse information creatively and imaginatively in seeking solutions to political problems and challenges.

Module Title: Penology
Module Code: LW545
Learning outcomes written by Dr Shane Kilcommins

On successful completion of this module students should be able to:

- Differentiate between criminal law as paper rules and criminal law in action.

- Outline and trace changes in punishment over time.

- Identify the determinants which shape punishment in late modern society.

- Employ different theoretical approaches to criminal law phenomena.

- Examine the extent to which such theories can explain occurrences in late modern Irish society.

- Interpret Irish criminal law cases, statutes and policy recommendations in socio-legal terms.

- Connect changing values and sentiments in punishment with a changing emphasis on criminal law and procedure.

- Assess current criminal justice policies in terms of direction and impact (as it relates to accused, victims, agencies and politicians).

- Question the extent to which criminal law really is objective and value free in orientation.

Module Title: Environmental Microbial Genomics: the role and ecology of microbes in the environment
Module Code: MB3005
Learning outcomes written by Dr John Morrissey

On successful completion of this module students should be able to:

- Outline the major classes of microbiota present in natural ecosystems.

- Explain how the physical, chemical and biological environment influences microbial activity.

- Describe, using examples, different types of ecological interactions involving microbes.

- Explain the general importance of microbial communities for ecosystem function.

- Describe, compare and contrast the methods that can be applied to study microbes and microbial communities in the environment.

- Explain, using examples, how diverse methods can be applied to understand microbial function in natural ecosystems.

Module Title: Methods in Microbiology
Module Code: MB3016
Learning outcomes written by Carmel Shortiss

On successful completion of this module students should be able to:

- Identify the steps required to complete each experiment individually and in a group.

- Define the individual steps required to complete the experiment.

- Arrange the steps in sequence so that the experiment can be completed.

- Organise the reagents, cultures, media etc. that are required for the experiment.

- Maintain a clear scientific record of each experiment and the data generated from the experiment in a laboratory notebook.

- Evaluate the data received individually and in a group discussion.

- Identify, individually and in a group discussion, the conclusions that can be drawn from the data.

- Present the completed experiment in a written report.

- Present the completed experiment in an oral report, identifying the outcomes of each of the steps above and paying particular attention to the conclusions.

Module Title: Managing Strategy and Change in a Growing Organisation
Module Code: MG5001
Learning outcomes written by Patrice Cooper

On successful completion of this module students should be able to:

- Discuss the major theories of strategic management and competition.

- Apply the principal strategy frameworks to case-based problems and recommend solutions.

- Critically evaluate the strategies being followed, the resources available, and the strategic options open to an organisation.

- Demonstrate management skills and abilities such as: negotiation, communication, project management, problem-solving and team work.

- Challenge the dominant paradigms in strategic thinking.

Module Title: The Child Health Research Project
Module Code: PC2007
Learning outcomes written by Dr Aileen Malone

On successful completion of this module students should be able to:

- Define research, differentiate between good and poor quality research using appropriate criteria.

- Formulate an original research question.

- Perform a comprehensive literature review.

- Identify and access bibliographical resources, databases and other sources of relevant information. Appreciate the strengths and limitations of different methods of data collection.

- Gather original data using the most appropriate research methodology.

- Recognise bias.

- Interpret research findings.

- Appreciate confidentiality and ethical issues.

- Communicate their research results appropriately in both written and verbal presentation.

Module Title: Unit Operations and Particle Technology
Module Code: PE 3002
Learning outcomes written by Dr John Fitzpatrick

On successful completion of this module students should be able to:

- Measure particle and powder properties, in particular, particle size, moisture content, particle density, bulk density, flowability/wall friction.

- For each operation covered:

  - Explain how each operation functions.

  - Identify the major variables that determine capital and operating costs.

  - Perform design calculations, where possible, to evaluate these variables. Where not possible, describe how to go about estimating these variables.

  - Perform experiments / small-scale trials to evaluate values of parameters used in design calculations (drying, filtration, fluidisation, silo design).

- Demonstrate an understanding of how particle properties and bulk powder properties influence production, storage, handling, separation and processing of particulate systems.

Module Title: Applied Thermodynamics & Fluid Mechanics
Module Code: PE3001
Learning outcomes written by Dr Edmond Byrne

On successful completion of this module students should be able to:

- Assess any pipeline system with respect to pressure differentials and fluid flow rates and design a pump-pipeline system for laminar or turbulent, single or multi-phase flow of Newtonian or non-Newtonian fluid through straight, branched or networked pipe systems.

- Select pumps appropriate for the range of process types encountered in the process industries.

- Categorise different rudimentary flow systems so as to employ Navier-Stokes equations which in turn describe these systems. Also demonstrate how these equations can be applied to more complex systems using Computational Fluid Dynamics software.

- Outline the nature of high velocity compressible flow and design a choked flow.

Module Title: Bioactive Natural Products - Pharmacognosy
Module Code: PS3005
Learning outcomes written by Dr Barbara Doyle-Prestwich

On successful completion of this module students should be able to:

- Identify the different classes of plant secondary metabolites.

- Explain the significance of the occurrence of secondary metabolites in different taxonomic groups, in different plant parts and in different locations around the world (the influence of the environment).

- Discuss the ethics involved in harvesting drugs from endangered plant species and the obligation on the harvester to local communities in that area.

- Design protocols for the up-regulation of secondary metabolites in plants using a biotechnological approach.

- Conduct laboratory experiments on phytonutrients (using titrations and chromatography) (and also using a genetic engineering approach for the modification of medicinally important plants).

- Write a 3000 word review article on a chosen relevant topic using published literature.

- Distinguish between the different available strategies for the ethical and sustainable use of natural resources.

- Use the information gleaned from the industrial visits to more fully evaluate the implementation of quality control systems for the extraction of natural plant products on an industrial scale.

- Defend the use of rare plant species for human therapeutic purposes.

Module Title: Restorative Dentistry
Module Code: RD3003
Learning outcomes written by Dr Edith Allen

On successful completion of this module, students should be able to:

- Examine a patient extra-orally and intra-orally.

- Formulate an appropriate treatment plan based on an understanding of the disease process present and a prediction of the likely success.

- Identify dental caries and restore a tooth to functional form following caries removal.

- Record an accurate impression of the mouth and identify all anatomical features of importance.

- Design a partial denture with appropriate support and retention.

- Administer successfully and in a safe manner with minimal risk to patient and operator, infiltration and regional nerve block anaesthesia.

- Communicate with patients and colleagues in an appropriate manner.

Module Title: Comparative and Animal Physiology
Module Code: ZY3011
Learning outcomes written by Dr Sarah Culloty

On successful completion of this module students should be able to:

- Describe the main components of the immune system.

- Compare the immune system of vertebrates and invertebrates.

- Contrast the immune system of vertebrates and invertebrates.

- Evaluate the effectiveness of the different mechanisms used by parasites to evade the host's response.

- Demonstrate the practical skills required to detect and measure components of the immune system.

- Defend the findings obtained in the laboratory practical in a scientific paper.

References

Adam, S. (2004), *Using Learning Outcomes: A consideration of the nature, role, application and implications for European education of employing learning outcomes at the local, national and international levels.*
Report on United Kingdom Bologna Seminar, July 2004, Herriot-Watt University.

Allan, J. (1996), Learning outcomes in higher education, *Studies in Higher Education,* 21 (10) p. 93 – 108.

Anderson, L.W., & Krathwohl, D. (Eds.) (2001), *A Taxonomy for Learning, Teaching and Assessing: A Revision of Bloom's Taxonomy of Educational Objectives.* New York: Longman.

Biggs, J. (2003a), *Teaching for Quality Learning at University.*
Buckingham: Open University Press.

Biggs J. (2003b), Aligning teaching and assessing to course objectives. *Teaching and Learning in Higher Education: New Trends and Innovations.* University of Aveiro, 13 – 17 April 2003.

Bingham, J. (1999), *Guide to Developing Learning Outcomes.*
The Learning and Teaching Institute Sheffield Hallam University, Sheffield: Sheffield Hallam University.

Black, P and William, D (1998), Inside the Black Box: Raising Standards through Classroom Assessment, London: Kings College.

Bloom, B. S., Engelhart, M., D., Furst, E.J, Hill, W. and Krathwohl, D. (1956), *Taxonomy of educational objectives. Volume I: The cognitive domain.*
New York: McKay.

Bloom, B.S., Masia, B.B. and Krathwohl, D. R. (1964), *Taxonomy of Educational Objectives Volume II: The Affective Domain.* New York: McKay.

Bloom, B.S. (1975), *Taxonomy of Educational Objectives, Book 1 Cognitive Domain.* Longman Publishing.

British Columbia Institute of Technology (1996), *Writing Learning Outcomes,* British Colombia, Canada: Learning Resources Unit.

Brown, S. (1999), Institutional Strategies for Assessment.
In Brown, S. and Glasner, A. (Eds), *Assessment Matters in Higher Education.*
Buckingham: SRHE and OU Press.

Brown, S., and Knight, P. (1994), *Assessing Learners in Higher Education.*
London: Kogan.

Council of Europe (2002), Seminar on Recognition Issues in the Bologna
Process, Lisbon, April 2002. (http://www.coe.int)

Dave, R. H. (1970), *Developing and Writing Behavioural Objectives.*
(R J Armstrong, ed.) Tucson, Arizona: Educational Innovators Press.

Dawson, W. R. (1998), *Extensions to Bloom's Taxonomy of Educational
Objectives,* Sydney, Australia: Putney Publishing.

Dillon, C and Hodgkinson, L (2000), *Programme specifications in a flexible,
multidisciplinary environment*, Quality Assurance in Education, 8(4), pp 203-10

Donnelly, R and Fitzmaurice, M. (2005), Designing Modules for Learning.
In: *Emerging Issues in the Practice of University Learning and Teaching,*
O'Neill, G et al. Dublin : AISHE.

ECTS Users' Guide (2005), Brussels: Directorate-General for Education and
Culture. Available online at:
http://ec.europa.eu/education/programmes/socrates/ects/doc/guide_en.pdf

Ferris, T and Aziz S (2005), A psychomotor skills extension to Bloom's Taxonomy
of Education Objectives for engineering education.
Exploring Innovation in Education and Research, March 2005.

Fry, H., Ketteridge, S., Marshall (2000), *A Handbook for Teaching and Learning
in Higher Education.* London: Kogan Page.

Gosling, D. and Moon, J. (2001), *How to use Learning Outcomes and
Assessment Criteria.* London: SEEC Office.

Harden, R. M., Crosby, J. R and Davis, M.H. (1999a).Outcome-based education:
Part 1 – *An Introduction to outcome-based education,*
Medical Teacher, 21(1) 7 – 14.

Harden, R. M., Crosby, J. R and Davis, M.H. (1999b), *Outcome-based education: Part 5 – From competency to meta competency: a model for the specification of learning outcomes,* Medical Teacher, 21(6) 546 – 552.

Harden, R. M. (2002a), *Developments in outcome-based education.* Medical Teacher, 24(2) 117 - 120.

Harden, R. M. (2002b), *Learning outcomes and instructional objectives: is there a difference?.* Medical Teacher, 24(2) 151 - 155.

Harrow, A. (1972) *A taxonomy of the psychomotor domain - a guide for developing behavioral objectives.* New York: David McKay.

Jenkins, A. & Unwin, D. (2001), *How to write learning outcomes.* Available online: www.ncgia.ucsb.edu/education/curricula/giscc/units/format/outcomes.html

Krathwohl, David, R. (2002), A Revision of Bloom's Taxonomy: An Overview. *Theory into Practice,* 41 (4).

Mager, R. F. (1984), *Preparing instructional objectives.* 2nd ed., Belmont, California: Pitman Learning.

McLean, J and Looker, P. (2006), University of New South Wales Learning and Teaching Unit. Available online: http://www.ltu.unsw.edu.au/content/course_prog_support/outcomes.cfm?ss=0

Moon, J. (2002), *The Module and Programme Development Handbook.* London: Kogan Page Limited.

O'Neill, G. (2002), *Variables that influence a teacher versus student-focused approach to teaching*. UCD, Centre for Teaching and Learning report.

Osters, S and Tiu, F. ( ), Writing Measurable Learning outcomes. Article available on: http://www.tamu.edu/qep/documents/Writing-Measurable-Learning-Outcomes.pdf

Ramsden, P (2003), *Learning to Teach in Higher Education,* London: Routledge.

Shuell, T. J. (1986), Cognitive conceptions of learning, *Review of Educational Research,* 56: 411-436.

Simpson, E. (1972), *The classification of educational objectives in the psychomotor domain: The psychomotor domain.* Vol. 3. Washington, DC: Gryphon House.

Toohey, S, (1999), *Designing Courses for Higher Education.* Buckingham: SRHE and OU Press.

Website References

1. Details on Bologna Process: http://www.bologna.ie

2. Berlin Communiqué 2003:
   http://www.bologna.ie/_fileupload/publications/BerlinCommunique.pdf

   Bergen Communiqué 2005:
   http://www.bologna-bergen2005.no/Docs/00-Main_doc/050520_
   Bergen_Communique.pdf

3. American Association of Law Libraries:
   http://www.aallnet.org/prodev/outcomes.asp

4. University of New South Wales Learning and Teaching Unit.
   Available online: http://www.ltu.unsw.edu.au/content/course_prog_
   support/outcomes.cfm?ss=0

5. Quality Enhancement Committee, Texas A and M University, USA.
   Available online:
   http://www.tamu.edu/qep/documents/writing_outcomes.pdf

6. Tuning Educational Structures in Europe:
   http://tuning.unideusto.org/tuningeu/

7. University of Central England Educational and Staff Development Unit:
   http://lmu.uce.ac.uk/OUTCOMES/UCE%20Guide%20to%20Learning%2
   0Outcomes%202006.pdf

   http://lmu.uce.ac.uk/outcomes/#4.%20What%20are%20the%20benefits
   %20of%20Learning%20Outcomes4.%20What%20are%20the%20benefit
   s%20of%20Learning%20Outcomes

8. The University of Manchester:
   http://www.cs.manchester.ac.uk/Study_subweb/Postgrad/ACS-CS/
   webpages/syllabus/acs/ACS_AIMS.php

9. Dr Ann Ledwith, University of Limerick:
   http://www.ucc.ie/en/SupportandAdministration/
   ServiceandAdministrativeOffices/QualityPromotionUnit/
   LearningOutcomesConference/Presentations/DocumentFile,15075,en.pdf

10. Bridgewater State College:
    http://www.bridgew.edu/AssessmentGuidebook/chapter4.
    cfm#course_mapping

11. University of Wyoming:
    http://uwadmnweb.uwyo.edu/acadaffairs/assessment/Docs/Cap_2.doc

12. Rubrics – Monmouth University:
    http://its.monmouth.edu/FacultyResourceCenter/rubrics.htm